ALWAYS LOOKING BACK

SELECTED POEMS

by

Nancy Keating

PANGAEA

Saint Paul

ALWAYS LOOKING BACK

To Tom, and all the poets

International Standard Book Number (ISBN)
978-1-929165-61-2

Front cover photograph by Patrick C. Keating

Back cover photograph by Carol Hefner

10 9 8 7 6 5 4 3 2

Manufactured in the United States of America

Published by

P A N G A E A
www.pangaea.org

First Edition 2010

CONTENTS

Mortals

Terrains

ACKNOWLEDGMENTS

Grateful acknowledgement is made to the editors of the following journals, anthologies, and websites in which these poems first appeared, sometimes in a slightly different form:

Xanadu, "August Night, Brightwaters"
Mad Poets Review, "Tupperware Days: A Memoir" and "United Nations"
Abbey, "the waxing"
Bellowing Ark, "Friday at the Paradise," "In San Sisto's"
Pegasus, "My Animals"
Drown in My Own Fears, "I want her life"
Hidden Oak, "Vision Quest"
Barbaric Yawp, "Emma"
Poetyr, "Stealth"
Main Channel Voices, "How It Happened"
Iodine Poetry Journal, "Montpellier"
The Sow's Ear Poetry Review, "Love Story"
JAW Magazine, "It is the trance of knowing"
The P.E.N., "Native Plants" and "Lunch, Mid-August 2001"
Long Island Sounds Anthology (2008), "In the Shower," "It is the trance of knowing" and "Your Voice"
Long Island Sounds Anthology (2009), "For Patrick Stewart, After Seeing Macbeth," "Perspective" and "To Not One but Several Exes"
Writing Outside the Lines: An Anthology, "Pink Shirt"
Website of Maxwell Wheat, first Nassau County Poet Laureate, "The Future Shape of Poetry"

"Snow at Night" was part of Simplicity, an all-media members' show mounted by the East End Arts Council. It also appeared on the Website of Maxwell Wheat.

"A Garden in Babylon" received Honorable Mention in the Princess Ronkonkoma Productions 2008 poetry contest.

NK

Reflections

ALWAYS LOOKING BACK

Weekends, I approach my yard with tools
and a mission, meaning to find:
Amelia Earhart. Meaning. Peace of mind.
Bits of my lost selves:
The ponytailed five-year-old
whose black Scottie
(my first love, silky black with his
best-dressed red-and-green plaid belly)
slid down between the bed and the wall
of an Ontario bed-and-breakfast.
The quote-ruby-unquote birthstone ring that
squirmed out of a tote bag at Cedar Beach.
The sunhat from Korvette's that an August breeze
scooped out from the trunk
of our white Plymouth Valiant—
it had a push-button transmission—
at the old Orient Inn. (It had been
quite the glamorous hat. Once, the inn
had been glamorous too.)
Flotsam from
the South Shore's last safe childhood,
places and things that we leave
or that leave us. Like the last Christmas present
from my mother, the bracelet I slept in
till waking one morning to an empty wrist.
It must be here somewhere,
the last token of someone's love,
maybe my last token of love, period.
A memory and a fear, all here.
I rake the driveway, sifting in gravel,
panning for gold.

CABINET OF IMPERFECT MEMORY

the drawer of not-quite-perfect memory
slides off its track when you
yank at it, but it yields to you a
paradise – overstuffed –
of those perfect report cards you
lost on the way home
of the best not worst not boring parts
of any lover you had or wished
to have
of friends and family no longer dead
who spill out onto the old
linoleum floor
jump up and kiss your face
for once as free of doubt as dogs

THE GEOGRAPHY OF LOSS

is an old and still and very big thing,
a geography of flatness and lacks
like for one a lack of elevation
its markers show no real movement
enabling one to map it
here a glacial moraine of
small emotional pitfalls
there abruptly a lake without bottom or beach
no waves of grief to erode its shoreline
no dizzying peaks of hysteria
no treelines outside the city of ghosts
a metropolitan area of the missing
beyond plains of dimly remembered
pain under the longitude-latitude grid
denoting degrees of emptiness the only movement
underground streams of sorrow
coursing beneath the stasis of pine barrens
ringed by phragmites
those cockroaches of the marsh
doing what they do best:
filling in the empty patches
and the grey ribbon roadways
tie place-name to place-name
with more verve than the bereaved
the volcano is spent
there will be no lava

THE WAXING

when you unwind the tar and burlap
from your one fig tree

face it   you're less
than impressed only a fingernail scratch

along a branch tells you
this cluster of twigs remains robust

it's an analog world
not digital

parsing changes in more or less
not yes and no

you need to look close amid the gray
and brown detritus of fall and ah

there they rise up   blue tapers of crocus
their leaves shaming the grass

lethargic refusing to be goaded
basically copping an attitude

of go on without me
I'll be along later

birds are brown and busy
hear them partying in the bushes

SOME THINGS ONLY HAPPEN ONCE

Why does it always feel like always
when you only made snow angels,
three of them, exactly once
and there was only one barbecue
at your piano teacher's house
and your father only took you once
to meet his great painting buddy
in that old summer cottage down
Fire Island Avenue
and they drank scotch and you
drove home while he made
rude remarks about that man's wife.
And back in grad school in Minneapolis
you only had to fight off one woman
who thought the love of
your med-school boyfriend
would be the better deal.
Then you left him anyway.
And here's one: Why does
losing one stuffed animal at age five
right before your family moves back
to the home you were too young to remember
translate to years, I mean years of therapy?
Those 50-minute hours, over and over.
Well. You only kissed one rock star,
all right, he was a Canadian folk star
and he was short and it was really kind of a
letdown.

And it was only the one time,
you only rode once along
Shepard Road in St. Paul,

a little coked up, hanging onto
that skinny younger guy Joe on
his farting old Moto Guzzi
in his hot black leather jacket
and you also dressed to kill
the hissing Mississippi
and the mysterious caves
in the bluff beyond
to your right,
the good people of St. Paul
in their Craftsman houses
up Ramsey Hill to your left,
sensible and sleeping up there because, well,
because they were old and probably
married or shacked up
and definitely not riding, riding
with their faces into the wind
screaming a conversation back and forth
to see some guy play at a club
near where Shepard Road pours itself out
at West Seventh Street near Lowertown.
They could never get the joke that kids
couldn't help themselves year after year
hoisting up to that Schmidt Brewery sign
out there by that old High Bridge,
no idea how they did it over and over
knocking out every second neon letter
for the good people of St. Paul to read,
assuming they ever found themselves
out of bed some night and
tearing east along Shepard Road on back of

a bitching vintage Moto Guzzi.
And you were so scared and happy
and he was mad bad and dangerous
and so were you
and you hadn't even slept with him yet,
Joe, that is,
and in fact you never did.
A couple months later he wanted to.
No Moto Guzzi, right then, no,
just a guy who you saw would
hit bottom in a year, tops,
and the sad white briefs.

STEALTH

My house knows that I can't bring myself
To vacuum every week, and there's
A thing it's counting on. My house sheds
Particles like dandruff. Brain cells breed
In corners in the dark. Recriminations collect
In between each screen and windowpane.
Never mind that my carpenter ants
Eat well but pay no property taxes,
That dry rot comes to the damp places.
No, we're talking alien forces here.
The baby I never had has turned in on herself,
Heckling me from up by the ceiling-spider.
The soul-mate I thought I'd found stood me up
For dinner last month. In photos, my beauty
Has extruded someone's grandmother
Into the spot I occupy between friends.

THE FUTURE SHAPE OF POETRY

To accommodate the demands of a changing world,
we have evolved. The lyric has died a justifiable death.
We no longer need meter.
We're through with rhyme.
We are poets without obvious music.
We have arrived at the far shore
where one ponders a whole new movement
to replace post-postmodernism.
Maybe we'll just call it typing. Or rather,
keyboarding. Like the old electric Underwood
you give to the e-waste recycling company,
the paper we bundle up and throw to the curb,
everything we once absorbed and chanted
is old-hat. "Old-hat" is old-hat.
The old ones, the ones who rhymed and counted,
used to call it prosody, but
we have evolved. It's so freeing. In fact,
I'm thinking of evolving us still further
along the distance between them and us,
tipping the whole concept of meaning overboard.
Reality, the Is of the universe,
is overrated as it is. We have evolved
beyond these cheap tricks. Time to get serious.

THE LAST WORD

cancer is the root of all evil
another cancer, another dollar
X marks the cancer
there's no cancer like home
any cancer of yours is a cancer of mine
cancer doesn't grow on trees
cancer can't buy you happiness
cancer makes the world go 'round
(money makes the cancer go 'round)
there's a pot of cancer at the end of the rainbow
there's cancer in them thar hills
worth its weight in cancer
you scratch my cancer and I'll scratch yours
a fool and his cancer are soon parted
a cancer saved is a cancer earned.
he who lives by the cancer shall die by the cancer
you're burning the cancer at both ends
better the cancer you know than the cancer you don't know
a cancer divided against itself cannot stand
put your cancer where your mouth is
I haven't got a cancer to my name
cancer springs eternal
there's light at the end of the cancer
life is just a bowl of cancer
go out in a blaze of cancer
the cancer's in your court now
time flies when you're having cancer
another day, another cancer
money is the root of all cancer

IN THE SHOWER

The cunning way skin slips away from bone,
like with a well-cooked goose,
you notice it yourself, scouring your shifting back
in circular massaging strokes of care and blindness.
Soap is your concern, your holy demonstration
of purity and self-regard,
pandering to the youth that is leaving
so gently you barely sense the backward wave,
writing you a "dear Jane" postcard,
you with winter now coming on,
burying yourself in damp steam and flannel,
wrapped up too late in glad worship of the flat belly,
the clear innocent eye,
as he, he vaguely sketches a goodbye
from that bright unreachable resort by the water.

IT IS THE TRANCE OF KNOWING

It is the trance of knowing
It is the bones of codebreakers
The instinct of bats
The touch of the blind

It is the caress of sensing
It is the familiarity of grandmothers
The noses of dogs
The nerves of the deaf

It is the long history of watching
It is the terrain of gardeners
The comprehension of owls
The Braille of the lover

FOG IS A POROUS FENCE

fog sits over the golf course daring the more determined duffers to
   shank that ball and then find it again in the rough

fog smudges the edges of tall spindly trees like a partially erased
   drawing by a little girl who has a set of new pastels

fog colors the whole coastline with powdery silvery grey dove grey
   mockingbird grey spelled g-r-e-y in the English way because that's
   where fog lives most of the time

fog makes evergreens less green, moss a little less ugly as it climbs up
   trunks of old maple trees

fog has no agenda or malice

fog is seductive

fog pillows the road

fog carries with it a plan for the ghosts of everyone who has ever been loved

fog is God's way of inviting the sky to sit on the ground and rest awhile

fog is the scrim between the short term and tomorrow

fog quiets people down slows them down injecting the most harried
   among us with an unfamiliar yen towards contemplation

fog is the spun pewter of the bay and sea making themselves known to
   the waterfront café crowd at happy hour on a Sunday afternoon

fog is a pigeon

fog suspends its aura over the main road through the older suburbs

fog transports Ussé, the Sleeping Beauty castle in France, through the
   magic of childhood fairy tale powers to a place down the street
   in your memory where the black swans are forever swimming in
   the moat and even though you were with your husband at the time
   you immediately got a crush on the French tour guide in his navy-
   blue sweater and thin nose and deep brown eyes you hoped he was
   noticing you and you should know that yes, he did

fog hides the outside world from you until you are ready to go back to it

IN THE CARD SHOP

You know, all this
free-floating prefabricated love
really takes my breath away.
Since everybody died
or left, I had forgotten
all the reasons why people
buy all these occasion cards.
Some women, and it is mostly women,
are card people. Not me, especially;
never was. And yet,
it's always good to know
that for a price
you can buy happy upbeat words,
just in case, temporarily,
you're fresh out of them.

STERILE KANGAROO

I have my mother's big feet.
She is gone and I miss her,
now that she is gone
to wherever roos go
and knows everything,
something they say of all the dead.
I can no longer crawl into her pouch
and feel warm and one with her
as we bound across the savanna
racing the cassowary,
or hop to riverbank and grassland.
Who will protect me from
these dingos and cats,
and laugh with me at
the laughing song of kookaburras?
And none will issue out of me,
I know now, alone and erect,
facing the shotguns of men
out for meat and leather,
with my big proud feet
and my marsupial pretensions,
a beast with more past than future.

MEMO

The memo has grown a personality.
Not a very nice one.
Thinks it is important.
Wears exclamation points
like big long drop earrings
that say Notice, Urgent.
Will only wear black and white.
Is trying to make some kind of
statement. It lies on the desk
vigorous as a dead fish
expecting a response, perhaps homage.
It was bleating something about budgets,
signatures, approvals, but really,
it could drop the attitude.
The damned thing wouldn't even be here
if I hadn't printed it out.

HOW TO VOTE

See who the *New York Times* likes.
Then pick the other one.

Find out which one finished most of
Moby-Dick. No one's gonna vote for that elitist.

Here's one: Get to the artist's colony in heaven.
Check out who Norman Rockwell's painting.

Find out which one likes football
And NASCAR. Mmmm, chancy.

Consider the whole thing about guns.
Which candidate actually has one? There you go.

Who is most likely to embarrass America
Before the world? There's our boy.

One has the better platform. One has snaky staffers.
Look at recent history. Think about it.

PRAYER

Our Lady of Good Haircuts,
Pray for us.
Our Lady of the Jimmy Choos,
Pay for us.
Our Lady of the Spas,
of the Nail Place,
of Good Credit,
Shop with us.
Holy Mother of Bod,
Stray with us.
Our Lady of the Hot Landscapers,
Queen of More and Better Sex,
Notre Dame of the Hunky Quarterbacks,
Um, intercede for us.
Our Lady of Miraculous Mettle,
Madonna of the Muscles,
Give us strength.
Our Lady of Perpetual Help,
Occasional Help,
Not Nearly Enough Help,
Hang with us.
Blue Icon of Byzantine Beliefs,
Blessed Sacrificial Virgin,
Babe of God's Most Divine Fantasies,
Lady of the Seven White Veils,
Immaculate Contradiction,
Be our girlfriend.

I WANT HER LIFE

that is your wife's life
not the globe-trotting hobnobbing life
of the urban chardonnay academic
not the good-hearted volunteering life
of the public gardener
not even the internet fame you get
with bios and headshots and
adoring magazine interviews
no actually all I really want
is the life she's shared with you
the 30 years sleeping with you
every night like spoons
your hands securing a together life
the way we always used to do
the 30 years of your voice in her ear at night
and not a sound in mine
the 30 years of you washing her back
the scratchy circular caresses
with loofah and foaming soap and hands
your hands again
you started that with me
remember?
I heard her read a poem about
you washing her back
that could have been my poem
instead of this one

VISION QUEST

Take tripod and camera and set out
on the photo-shoot of the truth.
You have made an appointment. Focus
and lighting will be key. Don't forget
to zoom in. Alternate shots might involve
a filter or two, some gauze
to not hide the truth exactly, but
rather pretty it up around the penumbra.
Take as many shots as you like.
Delete the ones you don't. Shoot
a few close-ups. Ask for a smile.
Truth has, for once, dressed up for you.
Take all angles and save it for later.

NATIVE PLANTS

On Labor Day the grand political sweep
of recent U. S. history plays out
in news reports that more and more put me
in mind of tabloids by the deli checkout.
Why follow CNN when my own analogies
grow rampant in the yard? At last I've gotten to
pruning my privet hedges, ambivalent
about this infiltration by hedge bindweeds,
these loveliest of vines, with their near-Shakespearean
bell flowers, pink and weak as Ophelia sliding underwater.
They break your heart, these little trumpets.
Whether weed or native plant is anybody's call.
And over here the honeysuckle, friend of bees
(and children sent out by fathers to pull weeds),
with its yellow drop of nectar I can still taste.
Neither one moves me to pull it out. But I ask myself
about the worth of plants you make no effort to acquire.
And then, they're vines, and sometimes vines
deal death, like politicians, choking hosts
whose waning strength supports their noble beauty.

CONTRAINDICATIONS

Things persist in going where
they should not be: ladybugs (protected species)
on the twelfth floor of the office,
weed-seeds in well-planned flowerbeds of
English formal gardens. The man with no sex drive
spurning his relatively-new wife in
the Hotel Malta in Florence. They stroll along the Arno
after dinner. She sees the lingerie shop,
the mistress-caliber lace garments
with no short-term usefulness she can fathom,
wonders if she should develop a fetish,
if loving the clothes of love might soothe her heart.

And then, there is the obverse:
Things that refuse to show up on command.
Winning lottery tickets, pricey reblooming irises,
peace on earth, lecherous men
who have at least the decency to treat for dinner
once or twice, say nice things about
your dead relatives in their photo-frames on the piano,
even pick you up from the car-repair place
before they try to do you the big favor.
And then, "What's the point of all this lacy stuff?"
What does show up, despite your fiercest wishes,
is junk mail, house dust, banality without end.

HOW IT HAPPENED

the names have been changed
to protect the innocent
the facts changed to shield the guilty
the climate changed to
disguise the location
the story changed to give it
form   shape   content
the motivation changed
to fabricate
the illusion of rationality
memories changed
to spare the sensibilities of
everyone involved
the data changed
to create
a more predictive model
opinions
changed just for the sheer
argumentative
hell of it
the truth changed
to replicate
bliss

Terrains

HAVE YOU SEEN THEM

Fluttering as if for takeoff, as if to achieve lightness:
Have you seen them?
White papers on the walls, on the glass doors of Penn Station,
small bits of masking tape on pillars,
all the photos, phone numbers, posters
(all concerts called off till further notice).
Paper dances, litter blows across the plaza,
swirls in vortices over the concrete
by the Madison Square Garden entry.
Have you seen her? Have you seen him?

We didn't know these people and now we never will.
They're gone into thin air.
Said goodbye one morning and didn't get home.
No one can believe it, how it all went down.
Their families still prayed that somehow
they'd turn up, at least some of them.

In the slanted sunlight of early autumn,
the pigeons poop in any old place, oblivious,
pecking at bits of bagel and hot-dog rolls,
the flying rats of New York,
while across Eighth Avenue, life goes on:
three-card monte men set up to fleece the tourists
in front of the post office where the entire world can read
its engraving about neither rain nor snow nor gloom of night
staying these couriers from the swift completion
of their appointed rounds.

FIRST HOUSE

You alone in your first house
you alone find the bones of a squirrel
its furry tail intact
patient and alone in the empty attic of your first house
and you alone make intermittent love with borrowed men
and you alone hear the nickering of ghost horses in the barn
and the cold sky hovers like a banker's suit
over your first house
and you alone understand what the barstool historians meant
when they spoke about your first house
and why it may be your last house too.
You alone are cognizant that it's 19 miles to Patchogue
and 78 miles to Springs from your first house
a half-mile from the train station
a decade away from tragedy
a distant remove of tears
and you are triangulating the distances between all that and this first house
where small maple trees grow in gutters
and mold is eating the plaster
and insects are eating the floorboards
and you alone paint walls and closets
shimmering flower colors in your first house,
and it's yours, all yours, your choice, your taste, your headache.
And your car radio plays the ambitious violin craziness of Bach's
    second partita
giving you agita as you pull away from your first house
down the red pebble driveway you love more than a person
leaving your house but only to do a few things that need doing
and then to return.
And you alone are evolving into who knows what
and you alone are nesting

finally in a place you found and chose all by yourself
and the house sparrows pause on the portico and flick their heads and wings
side to side
little and grey
chirp chirping and heedlessly alive and pleased to be so
and the mourning doves dodge and flush each other out of the privets
and coo in that call they make which sounds sad to our ears
but probably not to theirs
and the spring smell of dirt fills your lungs with its promise
and the sinews of grapevines look like your strong muscular grapevines
and they are
all yours
yours alone.

A GARDEN IN BABYLON

The redwood is a deciduous conifer,
a specimen tree in these parts,
a rarity with bragging rights. I have two.
As local legend tells, my parcel had
a racy past, risqué trade. Hugh, a local lawyer
now dead, described the Russian lady
who would put her trowel down, wipe her hands
down the flowered apron, reach into its pocket
and pay him for his newspapers.
"We all knew what Anna's business was,"
he'd say, and leer, and wink.
My tree service makes the redwood fifty,
which would be right, put there
by a lady who, whatever else she did
in life, knew her patch of dirt,
a trance-inducing garden that one
makes love to on one's knees,
a hard-won swain coveted by all who pass
in a small suburban village
no more nor less decadent than most.

GARDENER'S LAMENT

Here, the water is high
under the ground beneath my feet.
Here, tree roots will always
be shallower than inland.
On this piece of land
earth cops an attitude,
expelling hardy mums in winter.
The ground freezes up
and spits them out
like something distasteful.
And the trees? We'll just
always lose the trees,
right when they've finally
gotten to a decent size.
A hurricane will swing through
with its long arm
and swat them down.
Nothing wants to stay
where it's placed.
Sisyphus was lucky.

MY ANIMALS

She is not cuddly, this owl
who looks down from my barn roof,
standing on her mouse.
Like the snake, the mantises,
the several feral tabby cats
who stink up my flowerbeds,
stalk mourning doves, bask on my car.
Even the elegant quick fox
who tears across my driveway
at dusk, won't pose.
Certainly the possum does not,
as she glares from pinprick eyes
and waddles into my toolshed.
My toolshed, mind, missy.
This isn't Disney World, for sure.
My animals don't care to be my friend,
sing to me, give me advice.
They seem to not regard
me much, one way or the other,
nor realize who's boss.

JEWELWEED

You will not outsmart me, bitch.
You are like the gold-plated lead trinket,
the trashy souvenir of some other woman's
illicit weekend. You pale-stemmed
hollow shallow incubus,
horning in on my tidy bed,
spoiling every party,
drinking everything in sight,
fixing it so that
even throughout the roses,
lilies, iris and coneflower,
pink and cream and purple
your orange obscenity rears up throughout
clashing and interrupting
and everything is you you you.
Well.
Here's a newsflash, bitch:
this yard is mine.

DAY-LILY

What do we know about flowers?
Who will answer for me the question
of why, at the bend of my driveway
nestled up by a stockade fence,
what might be the last day-lily in the county,
a peach one, continues to put out petals
in late September?

Each weekday morning, I check out the window
as I back the car out, and there she is
(I think of her as a "she"), leaning over
at a drastic angle to catch the sun,
her one bloom up top, a half-dozen green buds
on the stem to back up my little show-off
who isn't quitting.

Let's call her Peachy. Kind of a defiant girl,
she wouldn't know that nature calls for cultivars
to be bred for looks and not longevity.
You'd expect more from her leggy orange cousins,
those all-Americans that grow along the highways,
but they're gone now. Peachy doesn't know her place.
She'll wither soon enough, we know;
no point in rushing.

CROCUSES

The times do not feel good.
Like a heavy-hearted queen
I lay my tarpaulin down
on icy-sodden October ground,
taking my isolated place
to minister to my regal lawn.
It is time to set the jewels,
blue sapphires of February hope,
as wind whips the sun away
once more, and chills the hand
that wields the conquering trowel.
Here I kneel in cold autumnal mud,
servant and protector of my lands
from the incursions of Nor'easters,
the rapaciousness of squirrels.
My shovel bites in, each hole
flooding with ground water. Globally,
the level of unhappiness rises. With
my bulbs, I plug leaks in the earth.

THE OLD WHOREHOUSE
FLOATS IN FOG

Caution, signal the yellow birches,
whispering *caution* in a morning
milk-white with fog. Rain or sun,
which way will the day go?
I stand, uncertain, keys in hand.
November, so of course maple leaves
thwap past my face, startlingly heavy.
But for the birch leaves—like the
wheels-for-hire of a parked taxicab—
the day is hard to see. Nor will I be able
to see the ghosts of the old denizens
of 20 Willow Street. A psychic
said she felt the spirits of
a lot of women here. I asked,
"Were they happy?" She said, indeed.
(Eyebrow wiggle.) I asked
what she saw the ladies wearing
and that's the point where she
flubbed her lines. I wonder what realm
they're working now,
right now, as my yard floats out of time,
not in the world at all, with the
yellow birch leaves rustling *caution*
out through the milk-white fog
and I see neither hydrant nor arriving visitor.

WHAT EVERGREENS ARE TRYING TO TELL US

If you could only tune your ears correctly,
if you had remained the contemplative type,
—and good luck with that!—
you would understand what your side yard
says to you, easily decode the nighttime message
of the yews, arranged like green velour pillows
now along banquettes of snow, who transmit—
not whisper—maybe something, oh, on the order of
get your coat on, come out, pat your hand on us,
we're not as cold as you might think,
you know you want to. Come out.
Or maybe even what you really wish for:
We quiet down the noise of outside for you.
We don't break hearts. We just are.
Come out and run your hands over us. If, as I say,
you could still hear what shrubs are not saying,
what they have been not saying for centuries,
you'd turn down the well-reasoned chatter of pundits
in suits, hair-splitting factoids they are passing
round and round, like political decanters
held this way and that up to the light.
You might shake loose from your wine-induced
bulb-catalog trance of thoughts that are not thoughts
so much as reveries of color you use
reading the junk-mail during the nightly news
to calm the anxious gardener inside who never
stops planting, chanting *must have must have*
and want and want and need need need,
am I pretty yet? safe yet? loved yet?

SNOW AT NIGHT

It's just snow,
yet a voice inside you
starts repeating *the beauty,
the beauty* like the heartbeat
of your insistent alter ego,
that little girl who wants you
to put her mittens on,
on a night still with snow
when the whole world,
the town, the street, the yard
and the sky all are soft-edged
and silver-lit and slowed
so quiet you hear yourself
think. And all you think is, *is
this the peace of death or
only hibernation,* but you don't
turn away from the window
and turn on the Weather Channel.
You stay with the peace,
snuggle down into it
like a cocoon, like the only afghan
Mom ever made (it took her years),
like the love of God
for the young and sweet.

FRIDAY AT THE PARADISE

pulling up to the South Shore roadhouse
not quite concealed by suburbs
place runs on beer and quarters
get me some, baby
let's roll us back some serious years
here in this fine juke joint not quite dive
feeding the best best jukebox around
you'll never think I'm a little cold again
and we will dance ... I mean dance...
cause I will be your juke-joint darling
Friday at the Paradise lounge

where were you to me back then back when
let's cast our old hormonal hippie minds back
to our separate seriously misspent youths
beer and quarters in front of a three-day weekend
watch me beat you at eight-ball
didn't know I could, did you?
you're gonna find I picked up lots of skills, sweetcakes
down through these years of trying to pass for normal
and I will be your shot-and-a-beer darling
Friday at the Paradise

we won't have no austere finale,
baby, ahead of three days off
what we're gonna have is a crazy absolute jumpstart
making out later down against the secretive trestle walls
the way we never used to do
get me more beer and quarters
I have a serious need for quarters
and I have a serious need for you, blondie
and we'll be more like who we were when we inhaled

41

keep feeding these quarters into that beat-up red neon jukebox
playing oldie singles by the old bluesmen
the old doo-woppers and songbirds
the old rockers who definitely inhaled
probably snorted and shot up too
but we won't care
they uncoiled their souls onto vinyl
and I will be your roadhouse darling
paradise at the Friday

and there was a time back then
when plywood bathroom doors were just fine with us
mystery carpet and nasty avocado walls
back before we got mature and got into worrying
beer and quarters are all we need
Friday night ahead of a three-day weekend
my suits in the closet
my jeans on my butt
your hands in my back pockets
and I will be your total paradise
darling at the Friday

AUGUST NIGHT, BRIGHTWATERS

You will have driven down these Norman Rockwell streets, Honda
windows rolled down, past mist rising up from the sweeping front
lawns of secure childhoods, moonlight kissing the wraparound
porches of love. You will have not seen but sensed the affection
behind coneflowers, black-eyed susans; the consideration of butterfly
plants, buddlea; the comfortable habit of rose-of-sharon shrubs; the
togetherness of hostas. You will have heard the tall rustling trees
speaking only to you, saying *ssshhhh,* saying *go deeper.* You will have
slowed to watch me behind glass, reading in a well-lit room, behind
the six-over-six windows of a Craftsman cottage, one of several
hundred in this impossibly real old suburb where everything that
used to be here still is here. You will have picked up a signal, *come
inside,* from the canteloupe glow of my lamps. You will have become
one with the choir of newborn cicadas who, shed their shells and are
vibrating for each other, one with the waning fireflies whose tentative
green bodies drift over the tall grass flashing their need. You will have
tried to call out *be with me,* hoping I read this.

APRIL, WEST SAYVILLE

Taking the curve by the golf course,
looking in the rear-view mirror,
and I'm alone. As usual.
Not so the cute couple
in the navy Toyota behind me.
She is driving, blonde, Jackie O
sunglasses. He rides shotgun.
He is handsome, of course,
like a Ralph Lauren model.
How unfair is that?
He takes her hand and kisses it.
And they are engulfed in their 6 p.m.
Saturday trance and don't know it
but we are together, all of us,
coursing through tufts of daffodils
surrounding us on Montauk Highway,
stealing glimpses of spring each from
the other, they not knowing that I saw.
And maybe soon,
maybe in my second springtime,
I will be finding the man
who kisses my hand
while I drive him to
wherever delight is,
and we all pull in to Oakdale
and the cute ones are crossing the tracks
and leaving me there with my hope.

WHAT YOU DESIRE

On Hill Street, in the small shop
that sits expectantly by itself
just as you enter Southampton (established 1640)
the spotty-headed antiques dealer
you have decided not to like
is overcharging for an eel spear,
presented to you as if it might be Neptune's
everyday trident, no doubt hoping
you will part with your money
for the experience of doing it
in this world-famous place,
or should I say venue,
where the dark lush leaves
rustle with money, where the air
is cleansed by money, where
the heedless breeze brushes past you
much like your own glancing awareness
of money. Or love. Or youth.

THE PROMPT

I. First Attempt

it's pressed into your hand
one rose petal, vermillion
you feel its color and in your knowing
you know what this is

yes I do
this is the test I'm gonna flunk
here we all are in France at this
writer's retreat
the dog ate my homework
and I would like to buy another prompt

because it's so not happening just now
I would like to be going for something oh
plangent and quivering and real
but all the other girls
and we're all girls
know each other from the workshop
in Brooklyn
and they're every one of them a size 4
not bereaved or just-divorced
they have people to phone and fight with
every night

what I'd really like to do is
drink wine go shopping
sit in that very pretty park
near beautiful downtown Montpellier
or maybe that other very pretty park
out by the aqueduct

or go again to the nice quite big church
for St. Roche, the bogus local saint,
kind of too bourgeois-built-by-bankers to be a big
French landmark but good enough for me
I mean we went there and it possessed me
I reworked my entire childhood
where my mother's name had been *maman*
and we'd walk down cobblestones to Mass
rather than driving to park on Long Island asphalt
and I grew up French and tasteful
with croissants every Sunday instead of poppy-seed rolls
and my ex-husband wore a muffler all the time
and smoked Gitanes instead of Marlboros
and was the quiet type

now that was a prompt

II. Second Attempt

oh no
look people, we're in France
and what do we get but rose petals
true enough we're outdoors
but we're "being creative"
here in a formal downtown park
with amazing flowers waving in the
Mediterranean breeze—got that the Mediterranean
which is right over there—gorgeous stalks
in the largest streakiest urns I've ever seen—
which nobody steals incredible to me—
making art out of this goddamn rose petal

fine

velvet as a cat's ear
warm to the touch
the softest of tensions
a right side and a wrong
doesn't last long
can't hold it forever

sure as hell
I'm mashing mine up
genius eludes me
why in hell did I spend all this money
so far I'm not thinner
or more creative
and we're only here for two more days

captured in pages of so many books

but not this one,
this damn rose petal is getting
just a tad soggy right about now

it has hundreds of names
so much and so many so rich
we know how it feels
like dessert or your kisses
anything you wanted too much

oh please, I don't even know the names
of the trees they have around here
I've just destroyed
a perfectly good rose petal
can't we just go get a brioche?

THE SPICE MARKET

eighty kinds of spices
on a table
I do not think
with prayer or thanking God
my chant is all too human:
give me give me
lavender to crush and smell
beneath my hand like the
love of my life like you
mint to taste
orange to bathe in
vetiver to scoop and feel
like you
this orgy of scents and senses
and wanting.
I want I want the chant
of wanting pounds inside my head

MONTPELLIER

the wind attacks from the south
and it parches the lavender
the olive leaves
the chamomile
overturning empty market baskets
as it breezes through

it curls the shavings of orange wood
curls the toes of couples about to be lovers
swirls round the Three Graces fountain
cures the ancient-looking aqueduct
out by the war memorial
and the allée
pitting the stone
piercing its hundreds of years and arches
ruffling the bougainvillea in the park
passing through

south wind stings the aging skin
of sensitive lady tourists
who heard about this place in school
drinking real French wine with that
older Vietnam-vet student they lost track of
who passed through like the rest

and who now at last can only lust
for the static well-organized
beauty one can pack or ship
to mount on foyer walls
of second homes upstate
and they too pass through and go

IN SAN SISTO'S

You are holding my hand in Como,
a dreaming city, soft with hard surfaces,
silk and chocolate and lace and stone,
in the quarter where three centuries
are nothing, where sunny days are dark.
Then I stop at a jeweler's window,
you trot into a bookstore and
the beggar appears, a gypsy, *zingere,*
and I know he's thinking *turisti.*
He could follow us, could take one of us.
Europe is old, the alleys know more
than we do. Get me out of here.
Shadows stretch out blue on the stones
a we duck into a secret church.

An altar to the Virgin, old and loved
and intimate, waits to the left.
She must have powers, this one, rich in
gold chains and bracelets on her neck,
silver medallions pinned to her cape,
gifts from those whose prayers were answered.
More yearnings, expectations, dreams
flicker and hope, four rows at her feet.
Light a candle, they tell children, and it
whispers your prayer over and over
till it burns out. Voices dance
on the stones behind and I wonder, What
should we ask for? What should the flame
keep repeating when we've gone?

THANATOURISM

I've almost died a thousand far-flung deaths
taken in water in the Chateau Marmont pool
pirouetted my car on the Intercoastal
skated toward thin ice in Kinderdijk (distracted by windmills)
crashed my plane before the cotton-candy Waikiki sunset
choked on a hand-poured dark chocolate in a café in Como
skied into a pine tree at Killington (aptly named)
O.D.ed in a suite at the Hotel del Coronado
picked up a little botulism at a bluegrass festival in Branson
poison from mercury-laced Cape Cod fish
danced off a bridge in Florence
saw a nipple beneath the poet's sweater
and just about had a stroke in Southampton
fell off the observation deck at Niagara Falls (aptly named)
pitched out of a gondola in Zermatt
put myself in a deep coma trying to write postcards
I'm half in love with what's called "easeful death"
still dying to know where is the fabulousness

GRAND TOUR

Unpacking in a Florence
hotel room,
in this Renaissance place
where every black-leather-clad
Vespa rider
has an ancestor in the Uffizi,
I wave the new pink
peignoir set
at my husband. The pieces
drift down in midair to a
strange mattress.
"Uh-uh, you won't get me
with that," he said.
Travel and learn.
One can drown in the beauty
of the made world, collecting
small hurts.

VISITING PHILLY AGAIN

The space feels different here. Stepping out
from the pub to the street, the space is different.
Maybe it's the terrain. It could be the elevation,
or the far distance from an ocean. Maybe the Amish
have something to do with it, or the ghost trains
at the Reading Terminal Market, the soft vowels,
the shoo-fly pie. Or Walnut Street, Maple Street,
the Rocky steps to the museum, the boat-houses,
or the Poe house off Spring Garden Street.
The first time I pulled in at the 30th Street Station
pigeons swooped down from rafters, tumbleweeds
of negligent air. Space again. I go to the Italian Market
fearful of running into the bastard long-haired artist
I liked to call my boyfriend, long ago.
He was looking for an affluent woman with tits
and no imagination beyond the good taste to read only
Penguin books. He actually said that: Penguin books.
He had a stutter. He moved Midwest. Space.

CAIRO

You do know about Cairo's
three subway lines
and big university
one stop before the Pyramids,
that the suburbs bump up against
the Pyramids,
that Cairo both is and is not
against Islam.

You do know about Cairo's
16 million soccer fans
and of course the river.
Most big cities have the river.

So you and I,
we think we know about
the river. My love, again
take my hand, again
let us cross it at night,
strolling to the opera house
just to see it, really,
but not to go inside.

We have more than 40 hotels
to choose from in this
dance of the decades, this
movable feast, this folly.
One thousand minarets
stab the sky here while you
stab my heart again.

So many times
we have met again.
We won't always have Cairo.
No matter. We've had New York,
Florence, Budapest, Paris,
cities with rivers.

THE INFINITE

Honeysuckle twines among the Concord grapes;
oak leaves twirl like biplanes toward the ground.

I am a hammock in fragrant darkness under the pergola
and you my weary old familiar traveler

who calls for me in the August of his years,
who comes around from the street to where I wait

back in the yard, swaying, and linden leaves are blowing
onto me, onto you. That's it; come lie down

and I'll cradle you under the old red stars
that died millions of years before you and I were born

and came to the awareness of each other.
In parsing the ways of love, there are no small ideas.

Mortals

LUNCH, MID-AUGUST 2001

On East 51st Street you face me
across a scuffed wooden pub table
for one lunch like all meetings
of all lovers, ineffable, religious,
painful, tacky, who can eat.
nervous, you knock the edge and
Bass Ale sloshes toward my purse.
God, you say, how come the tables
in these places always wobble?
They make them like that on purpose,
I say, so we don't stay here forever.
But please, let's never leave
this place, this trance,
you, tracing my wrist with your finger
saying, Look, I have a scar there too.
The guys drink their lunch
while we regard each other
by the wavy windowpane
and outside, the other guys
dump trash into a truck
making a racket, blocking traffic
in the clear early autumn sun
that seems to show reality so clearly—
the cutout beauty of the world,
of our story—
please God let us have a story
like my parents' 50-year story,
their first apartment still
right there on East 53rd Street
and I wonder, did they ever
wander into this old dive,

were they ever this dizzy,
and I've known you all my life
and today your eyes are green
and this table steadies me.

PAPIER-MÂCHÉ

Daddy could do anything
who else could turn our kitchen table
into a chrome-formica paradise
for making Christmas things

and Daddy was so fun
when we stirred up flour-and-water paste
and tore the *Long Island Press* into
long skinny shreds
and wrapped them round and round
the wire frames Daddy made

and beneath our gooey fingers
newsprint transmogrified into
round balls, boxy balls,
longer pointy-ended balls,
a strawberry with construction-paper leaves
a Santa with his painted eyes and lips
and cotton-ball brows and beard
—see how smart my Daddy was?

After our new decorations dried on the radiator
then we slathered on the poster paint
and gold speckly dots here and there
(green for the strawberry, of course)
while the Harry Simeon Chorale sang
their hearts out on the stereo

and I couldn't wait to show off
the ornaments Daddy and I had made
but they had to dry first
and we had to clean up the kitchen
before Mommy got home, darn it.

UNITED NATIONS

I could not play with them.
I arrayed them on my bookshelf,
moved them from here to there and back
and they were different
from each other and from me,
their native clothes glued on,
with rigid arms
and eyes that would not close
(no sleep, no ecstasy).
Blue and black
the Amish girl and boy.
The white plaster Japanese baby
reclined on his red cushion in ornate robes,
no diaper. The Dutch girl bald
under her swooping white hat.
Her shoes were wood, no laces.
The sari of the Indian bride doll
was gold instead of white
and had no lace.
And how to talk with them,
and in whose words?
And then the others call you strange,
not to be played with.
Better to do homework in the kitchen,
fragrant with meatloaf, Mom,
the radio and the warm forever dusk.

CHURCH BAZAAR

three girls went to Vegas paper leis round their necks
electric blue purple kelly green orange pink
over their navy uniform jumpers and bow ties
four dollars each from their mommies or six or ten to blow
never mind that all year round all Sister says is no no no
put the whole thing on the nickel wheel of fortune
and Colleen said This is really boss
and Patty said I don't know about this   Mom wants me to bring back change
and I said Look at the jewelry counter   rhinestone birthstones for a dime
and Colleen said These hot dogs are really gear
and Patty said I don't know they're made out of parts
and I said Look confetti on the floor   balloons
streamers   sunlight   can we stay all day
the old auditorium tarted up for a day and a night never so bright
with all the happiness a 9-year-old can take
and we flitted from booth to booth of temptation and sin
stepping on popcorn and broken leis and tangled-up streamers
in crazy color heaps on the old practical wood plank floor
and for once in our careful Catholic no no lives
the key word was yes yes to absolutely everything
and I bought rings and a pinwheel all-day sucker for the colors
and Colleen got a straw hat and a soda and gambled the rest
on the big whirring wheel and lost her school hat and laughed
and Patty said I don't know and kept her glasses on

TUPPERWARE DAYS: A MEMOIR

They always turned a little nasty,
spaghetti-sauce-stained, a little orangey,
showed every scrape of the knife.
The lids lost their new look,
then lost their grip—a lot like people, really.
It was a time when my mother
always dressed like Donna Reed, and
I would be helping Mommy match the lids
with the bowls, stack them neatly on the shelf,
fill them up with eight years of school lunches,
snacks and frozen O.J. in summer, or
Nana's prized recipe for chow-chow relish
the way they used to do in Canada.
And yes, it was the life we had,
alternating Richmond Hill and Flatbush
for the special days. Not the Norman Rockwell life,
exactly, but our own Irish-American suburban
iteration of those halcyon days and years,
the Sundays when the old ones played canasta
and passed around my Nana's shortbread
with the tea and Manhattans and Tom Collins,
when Grandpa lit up his pipe afterward
and claimed the television to watch "Gunsmoke,"
when holidays began with Wedgwood and ended
with wishbones and Tupperware and
goodbye kisses from blue-haired relatives,
and microwaves, like death, had no dominion.

PERSPECTIVE

"You only really need
five brushes," he said,
"fat down to thin.
But you have to clean
the paint off every time."
Dads are the ones
with the rules. The man
worked in insurance but
lived for painting. Never
owned a suit he didn't
ruin. Tried to make me
paint like him, sing like
him, be Irish like him.
Taught me how to
knock myself to others,
hide behind Mozart
and the Met and Monet,
look down on
Barbie and the Beatles,
be at once
above it all and less-than.
Daddy's little mini-me.
He collected weird
geezer friends, garage-sale
picture frames, tearsheets,
coffee-table books, museum
postcards. At the end
they put him in a wing of his own.

HYPOCHONDRIAC

she complained like a flute
in amateur hands
one note trilling over the last
the well-rehearsed organ recital
honed for years
fiddling with her bows
a tuba of farts at family holidays
a tremolo of self-pity
drumming thrumming away
any love she managed to orchestrate
with a final cacophony of mouth music
a pedestrian composition
starting yet and yet again

EMMA

She was a grave, artistic girl,
wrote a 9/11 poem
for the Sayville Rotary
to engrave on a monument.

There are preteen prodigies who
don't age well. In my morning paper,
a head shot of a spiky-haired teen
I don't recognize, a back story of meds and
talk therapy. Another one down
this year. I drink my coffee,
picking spent peony petals
off the floor. It could have been
legions of us, maybe
the anorexic, tightly-wound girls,
the sensitive, not-quite-present
girls, maybe the nerdy ones, needy ones,
just too romantic, or with
just too much vocabulary
and not enough smiling to hide
our all-too-obvious brains.

But we never scrambled up the bank
by the trestle over Blue Point Avenue,
turned,
faced the 3:40 out of Babylon
and whispered,
Get me out of here.

These petals I hold are post-peak pink
with rust spots just like blood.

EULOGY (FOR M.J.)

crows sit in bare tree branches in late afternoon
on the back road to Sag Harbor
coming from Babylon via Stony Brook
criss-crossing this skinny spit of salt and sand
putting miles and gallons of gas
between your death and my memory

this is an isle of length
but no distance will be far enough
and nobody will use the word "poignant"
to describe the way you died
or the blood or the smell or
the way you used to dress so carefully

I see the backs of strangers at
their dinner tables limned in golden light
following red of car tail-lights
to here, this new place with other friends
doing other things than drinking

we read to each other and somebody films it
for the archives of some university while
the sun goes down outside the old schoolroom
I feel like a bitch for saying I will forget you
as you forgot to care about anything but vodka
as you forgot to even try to live

SHOO-FLY

When I drove down to Philly
that weekend,
asking myself why I needed you
badly enough to make a road trip,
and then you acted pissed
that I'd woken you up at 1 a.m.
to be let into your loft,
and then when we went
for shoo-fly pie and
that couple snubbed you
on the sidewalk outside
the Reading Terminal Market,
well,
that should have been a clue.
Actually, two.

LOVE STORY

I have eight pictures of you, my latest man,
From one lunch in an East Fifties Irish dive.
Seven you posed for. In Photo #5
You're different, full-face, pensive.
In that flash between smiles, you were thinking:

This might be love. And one of us will hurt
The other, or we'll both do it,
Wound each other in this
Amniotic trance, this goofy state
Of unproductive lust. One of us will

Start finding fault. Then one won't phone.
One of us will have an organ out.
One will gain 30 pounds.
Some need I have will finally disgust her.
Some night we'll be too tired, angry, bored,

Distracted, drunk, and that will really be it,
Weeks of escalating digs, then
It will be over. We know too much, we two.
I look at you, that warm day in September,
A man in love in the worst possible way.

TO NOT ONE BUT SEVERAL EXES

I built a tower of money
tended a garden of sex
banked a fire of security
embroidered bedcurtains
in a pattern of children
put up and preserved
figs nuts pickles candied berries
fed my intellect on the arcane
my skin with the oil of second youth
inside and out all I
was did knew had
was calibrated to woo
and I will never get why
none of it was good enough for you

IF YOU LOVE ME

stop asking me how I looked at age 5 when I caught the mumps first
    on one side then on the other
stop trying to discover what countries I visit in my dream-state
stop using football and paradigm in the same sentence
stop buying figs and poker chips with your remarkable wallet
stop flaunting the clairvoyance of your immanent nose
stop throwing pomegranates like softballs into our neighbors' yard
stop moving to another continent right when we're about to get engaged
stop defending the artistic resonance of sculpture made overnight by
    small garden animals
stop denying me sex after we're married on ethical grounds
stop inviting soiled subway denizens over for dinner
stop kissing the backs of my knees in front of my mother
stop running for political office at the restaurant on Saturday nights
stop showing off your encyclopedic knowledge of dead religious fringe
    groups holed up in the crumbling eleventh-century fortresses of
    their own forgetfulness
stop telling anyone who will listen how unremarkable your felonies
    became over time
stop bringing me retrieved computer files containing evidence of the
    embarrassing past lives of people we have known up to now as friends
stop philosophizing about the pathos of used dental floss
stop isolating us on the kind of horrorshow island nobody ever retires
    to willingly
if you love me
there are certain behaviors that you will need to stop

LINES FROM A LOVE STORY IN SPACE

The weightlessness-control switch was broken, so lovemaking proved a challenge.

How high is up? So disconcerting when the concept of "overhead" means nothing.

She wished they'd chosen to go first class; it would be a very long trip and the bed had scorpions.

It occurred to her that they were really looking for heaven, the two of them.

Now he was critiquing the freeze-dried flowers from the ship's mess.

"Meet you at the intersection of Constellation and Gemini," he joked.

She had left the familiar world for him, and wondered if there were shopping, or fine dining, where they were headed.

They found out the hard way that Saturn City had a no-kissing-in-public ordinance.

"I'm over the moon over you," he said, and she realized how long a trip it would be.

The view out the window, all black and white, was giving her the Sirius blues.

Holding hands during both sunrises can only sustain romance for so long.

Here, when you want to leave, you take a capsule.

PINK SHIRT

You think I won't remember
what's underneath those oxford 2x2s,
those Brooks Brothers drapes and creases—
maybe you think you bought a WASP disguise,
that my memory can't touch you,
feel your shoulders' weight,
pull you onto me,
so
do it, beast
muscle your way down
these halls away from me,
go to that Thursday meeting.
Go on. I'm on to you.
High-powered, up-and-coming,
yeah yeah yeah.
Nice briefcase.
Nice stats.
Nice shirt,
goes with your complexion,
the blush of a fellow Catholic
who sinned with me
so happily and for so long.
Don't put your jacket on—
have mercy.
Now you want the straight and narrow,
you think you'll forget but
your shirt from Men's Furnishings,
17-32, so delectable,
will never save you now.
Take it off, beast,
and crunch it under my head.

YOUR VOICE

like a foghorn a half-mile out
like an ice pack on a bruise
like a jock calling plays at Thursday practice
like wind in my face
like a shallow lake with stones on the bottom
like cold rain in March
like a memory of leaves underfoot
like green apples
like some ghost
your voice in my ear

TO PATRICK STEWART,
AFTER SEEING *MACBETH*

For you
I would lose 30 pounds
get my veins done
maybe get some other work done
I would understand the rigors of fame
be the most interesting woman
you have ever met, ever
My subtle eyes would speak volumes
only to you when you're offstage
That *Vanity Fair* columnist would
Go on and on about what a perfect couple
we are and how the men with the talent
get all the luck and the good sex
I would shield you from the press
and weird fans who try to make you
notice them while you're working   .
(like my moron ex-husband
that time at *The Tempest*)
I would be the jet-setting
decorator of all our houses
I would buy you stacks of black turtlenecks
put them in all our houses
I would be whatever you desire
just as right now you are
the notepad I am writing on

PRAIRIE

if you were a prairie
and I were running out across you
navigating through your tall undulating grasses
like sea-waves on land
would you trip me up in a gopher hole
so a dozen foot-bones snap
or would you not

if you were a prairie
and I were to spark your notice
with the smolder I take everywhere
would you follow me
tear after me
with a fire that immolates the both of us
scorching our souls
or would you not

if you were a prairie
and I were calling out to the birds living within you
would you give up those birds to me
push them up to the sky at sunset
let me see them in the dusk
breathe your silvery prairie moan while they find each other
would you show me the shape and taste of you
make room for me in your fertile center
or not

MISLAID

where are those spoons
not in the drawer
not in my old trunk
never of course in the potting shed
the spoons you used to play as a party trick
the spoons you would chill in the fridge
and draw up and down my back
and the backs of my legs as we lay
lazily for hours in that ridiculous
off-campus room I was renting then
I mean those spoons
those particular spoons
for our tea
for our ice cream
for our one perfect year
so many pointless years ago
I know you didn't take them
and I find they're not here with me

THE ONE

Is this the way it starts in later life,
the old heart-song pushed aside by
watchful appraisal, weighing of Plans A and B?
You say hello in passing as I copy documents.
You seem remarkable as a shirt collar,
exotic as a Starbucks coffee cup,
distant as the ever-present hum
of ambient conversation around the building.
How could I ever lose you when the Internet
can find you, any cell-phone reach you,
any twerp tweet or text you (and you know they will)?
Are you the one I will love?

What I sense instead is a near-bureaucratic,
tedious, total lack of tension.
Even now, I force myself to whip up
some sense of suspense. Is it shared?
In what way are you regarding me?
We start with no continuity, no children
who look like you and me, no shared friends.
Portfolio not known. Scars, all, as yet unrevealed.
You pass the doorway to my committee meeting.
Twice. Has my stomach lost its memory of lurching?
Ah. There. Am I too spent to yearn?
Are you the one I will love?

KNITTING

Now that we have spun
these past and present hanks
and skeins of you and me,
I will make you into a sweater:
roll you, wind you unprotesting
into balls of yarn,
and take you length by length
between my two hands,
till all of you
has twisted through these needles
and become a finished thing
for me to wear,
a hundred thousand knits and purls,
your cabled chains running
up and down my front and arms
like a whispering wool cocoon.
I will inhabit you
at every point of me:
elbows, wrists,
collarbone, breasts,
swooning shoulders,
welcoming shoulderblades,
and we will be warm
heading into autumn.

WHY LOT'S WIFE LOOKED BACK

she left the stove on
left the fire on
left her lover on
led her lover on
left her lover ablaze
left her lover on the fire
she left her youth on the fire
she hadn't wanted to leave
had not wanted to leave her children
she forgot she had wanted children
she forgot she had children
she forgot everything
forgot to want
forgot to learn
forgot to yearn
forgot to gasp
forgot to breathe
she had forgotten to hold her breath
forgotten to keep her counsel
forgotten to keep her secrets
she had forgotten to hide her desires
forgotten all that she had wanted
the sweet spices of this world
forgotten what she was leaving behind
she had forgotten how to move forward
forgotten herself
forgotten her lot